Essential Dictiona Music Tl

G000057582

*Helpful music theory charts include
scales, modes, chords, key signatures and
a listing of instrument and vocal ranges*

L.C. HARNSBERGER

 # Table of Contents

Special thanks to Fred and Therese Harnsberger for all of their support.

COVER ARTWORK: *Timpani*—photo courtesy of Ludwig Industries;
French horn & saxophone—photos courtesy of Yamaha Corporation
of America; *Guitar*—photo courtesy of Richenbacker, Copyright
1995 Rickenbacker Corporation. All Rights Reserved.; *Violin*—photo
courtesy of Scherl & Roth and United Musical Instruments U.S.A., Inc.

Book design: Sue Hartman
Cover design: Carol Kascsak, Ted Engelbart

 Alfred Publishing Co., Inc.
16320 Roscoe Blvd., Suite 100
P.O. Box 10003
Van Nuys, CA 91410-0003
alfred.com

ISBN-10: 0-88284-766-X
ISBN-13: 978-0-88284-766-5

T H E O R Y

NOTES

o   whole note (semibreve)

♩   half note (minim)

♩   quarter note (crotchet)

♪   eighth note (quaver)

♪   sixteenth note (semiquaver)

♪   thirty-second note (demisemiquaver)

Terms in parentheses are those used in the United Kingdom and other countries.

NOTE RELATIONSHIPS

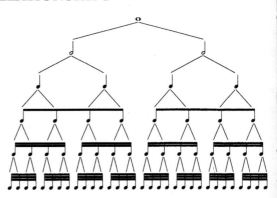

RESTS

▬   whole rest (semibreve rest)

▬   half rest (minim rest)

𝄽   quarter rest (crotchet rest)

𝄾   eighth rest (quaver rest)

𝄿   sixteenth rest (semiquaver rest)

𝅀   thirty-second rest (demisemiquaver rest)

Terms in parentheses are those used in the United Kingdom and other countries.

REST RELATIONSHIPS

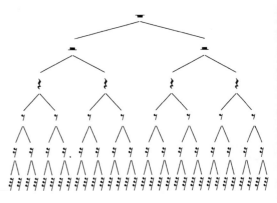

SCALE TYPES

⌣ = half step

⌐⌐ = whole step

⌐⌣ = whole and half step

Major Scale

Natural Minor

Harmonic Minor

Melodic Minor

Chromatic

Whole Tone

Pentatonic

MAJOR SCALES

A♭

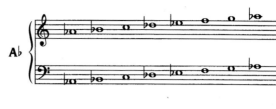

A

B♭

B

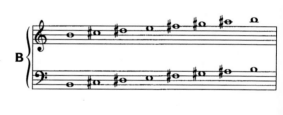

C♭

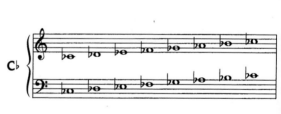

C

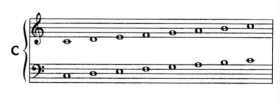

C♯

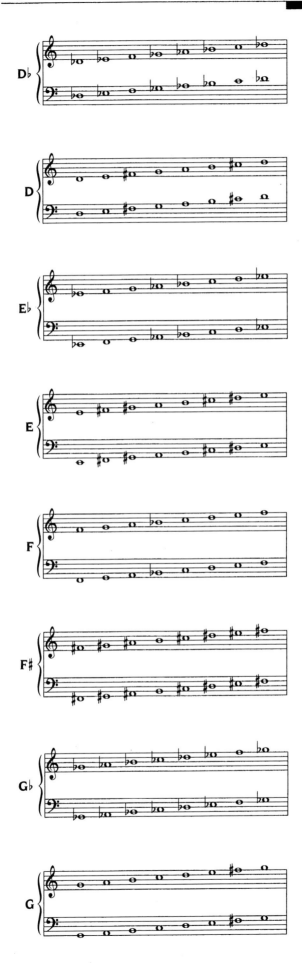

NATURAL MINOR SCALES

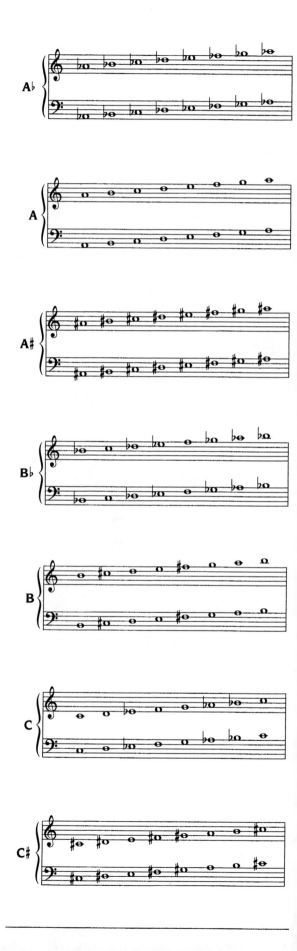

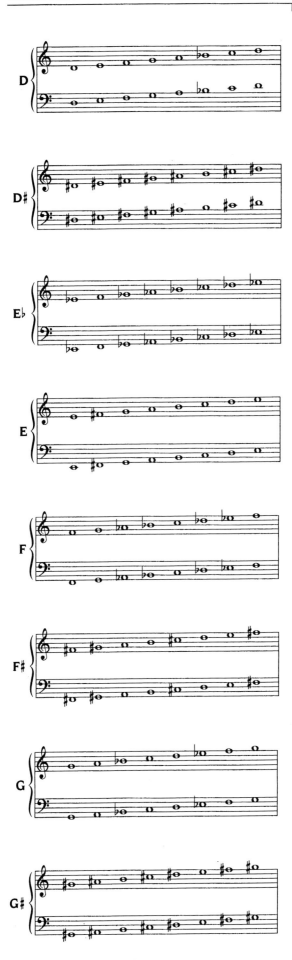

HARMONIC MINOR SCALES

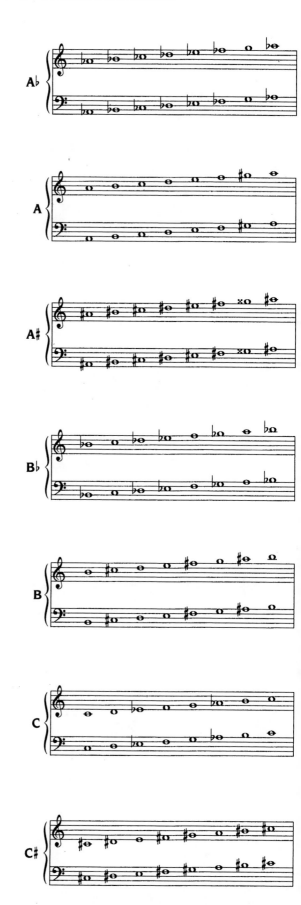

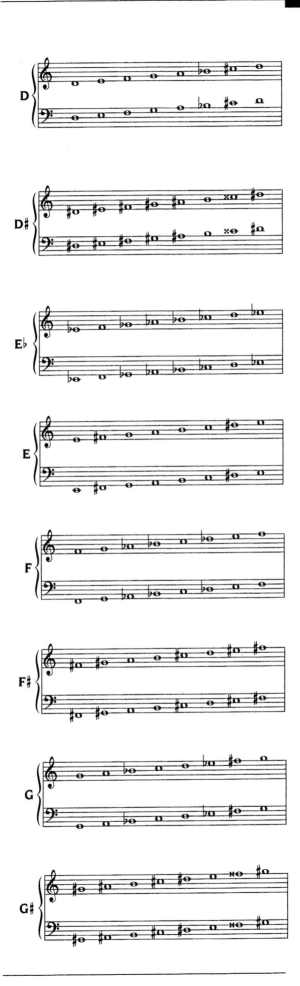

MELODIC MINOR SCALES

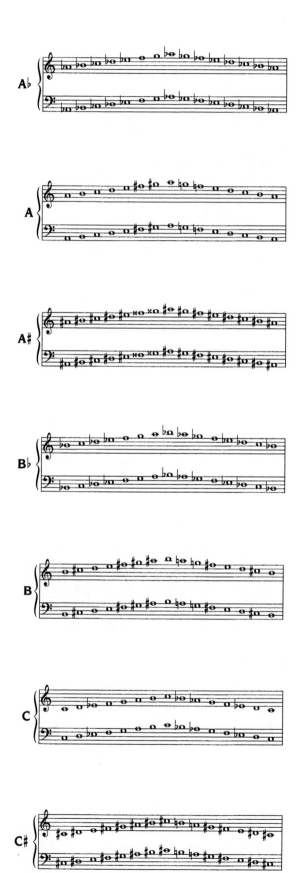

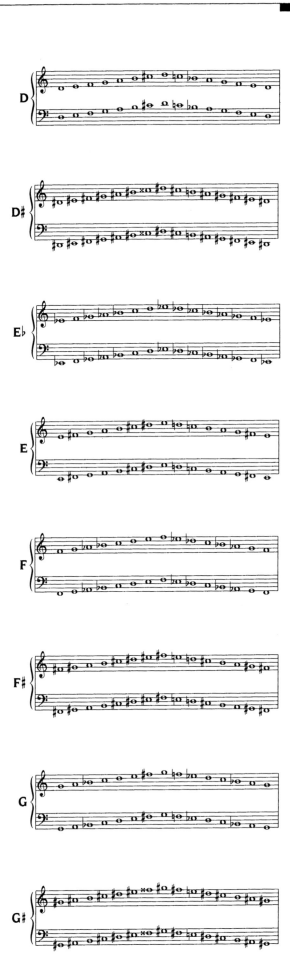

MODES

On the white keys
of a keyboard: Starting on C:

Ionian (identical to major scale)

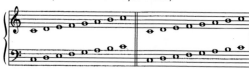

Dorian

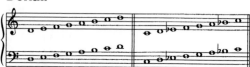

Phrygian

Lydian

Mixolydian

Aeolian (identical to the natural minor scale)

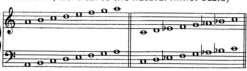

Locrian

ORNAMENTS

CIRCLE OF FIFTHS

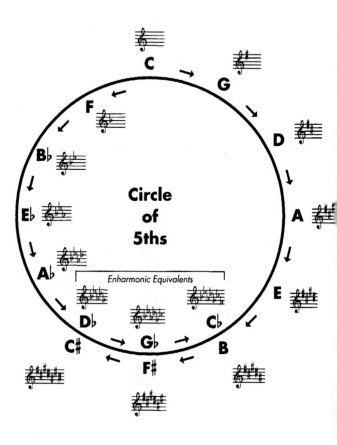

KEY SIGNATURES

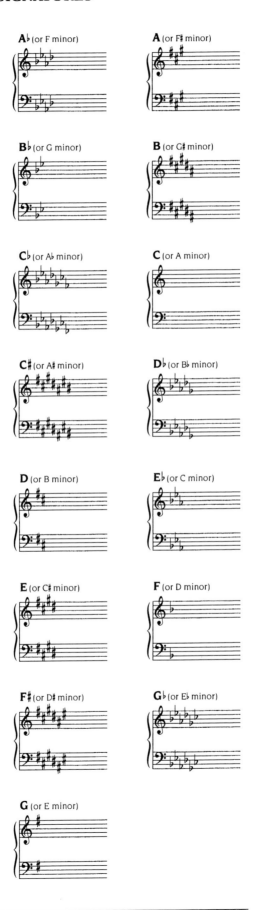

INTERVALS

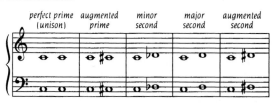

CHORD TYPES

Major
(root, major third,
perfect fifth)

Minor
(root, minor third,
perfect fifth)

Diminished
(root, minor third,
diminished fifth)

Augmented
(root, major third,
augmented fifth)

Dominant Seventh
(root, major third, perfect
fifth, minor seventh)

Major Seventh
(root, major third, perfect
fifth, major seventh)

CHORD CHART

DYNAMIC MARKS

pianississimo	***ppp***	Very, very soft.
pianissimo	***pp***	Very soft.
piano	***p***	Soft.
mezzo piano	***mp***	Moderately soft.
mezzo forte	***mf***	Moderatly loud.
forte	***f***	Loud.
fortissimo	***ff***	Very loud.
fortississimo	***fff***	Very, very loud.
crescendo	$<$	Gradually get louder (abbr.—*cresc.*).
decrescendo	$>$	Gradually get softer (abbr.—*decresc.*).
diminuendo	*dim.*	Gradually get softer.

MUSIC SYMBOLS

Flat	♭	Lower the note one half step.
Sharp	♯	Raise the note one half step.
Natural	♮	The note is neither flat nor sharp.
Double Flat	♭♭	Lower the note two half steps (one whole step).
Double Sharp	×	Raise the note two half steps (one whole step).
Fermata (Pause)*	⌒	Hold the note longer than its normal value.
Marcato	∧	Accented, stressed.
Accent	>	Play the note a little louder.
Staccato	.	Play the note short.
Staccatissimo	▾	Play the note as short as possible.
Tenuto	_	Hold the note for its full value.
Mezzo Staccato	᷂	Play the note short, but not as short as staccato.
Breath Mark	,	
Down Bow	⊓	
Up Bow	V	
Caesura	//	A sudden pause.
a due	*a2*	Both parts play in unison.
quindicesima	*15ma*	Play the note(s) two octaves higher.
all'ottava	*8va*	Play the note(s) one octave higher.
ottava bassa *8va bassa* [or *8va* placed below the note(s)]		Play the note(s) one octave lower.

* *"Pause" is the term used in the United Kingdom and other countries.*

TEMPO MARKS

Largo	Very slow and broad.
Larghetto	Slightly faster than largo.
Adagio	Faster than largo but slower than andante.
Lento	Slow.
Andante	A moderate graceful tempo.
Andantino	Slightly faster than andante.
Moderato	A moderate tempo.
Allegretto	Slightly slower than allegro.
Allegro	Fast.
Presto	Very fast.
Prestissimo	Extremely fast.
ritardando	Becoming gradually slower (abbr.—*rit.*).
accelerando	Becoming gradually faster (abbr.—*accel.*).

REPEAT SIGNS

Go back to the beginning and play again.

Go back to the repeat sign and play again.

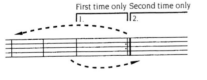

First time only   Second time only

Play 1st ending first time, repeat to the beginning, then skip 1st ending and play 2nd ending.

D.C. al Fine	Go back to the beginning and end at ***Fine.***
D.C. al Coda	Go back to the beginning and play to the coda sign (⊕), then skip to the **Coda** to end the piece.
D.S. al Fine	Go back to the sign (𝄋) and end at ***Fine.***
D.S. al Coda	Go back to the sign (𝄋) and play to the coda sign (⊕), then skip to the **Coda** to end the piece.

Repeat the previous measure.

Repeat the previous two measures.

GUITAR TABLATURE & NOTATION

Tablature is a system of notation that graphically represents the strings and frets of the guitar fingerboard. Each note is indicated by placing a number, which indicates the fret or finger position to be picked, on the appropriate string. For example:

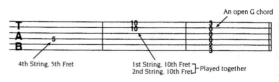

4th String, 5th Fret   1st String, 10th Fret ⎤ Played together   2nd String, 10th Fret ⎦

Arpeggio

Strike the notes of the chord shown from the bottom to the top. Quickly release each note after striking.

Bends

One- or Two-Note Up Bend: Pick the first note, then bend the string to sound up either one or two frets.

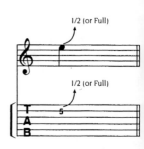

Pick Bend and Release: Pick the first note, bend the string up one or two frets to sound the higher (second) note, then straighten the string to sound the original (first) note again. Pick only the first note.

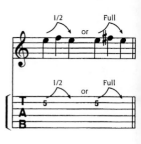

Bend and Then Pick: Bend the first note up one or two frets before picking it. This is usually followed by a down bend.

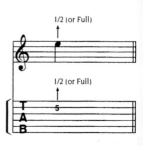

Harmonics

Natural Harmonics:
The fret finger lightly touches the string over the fret, and then the string is picked. A chimelike sound is produced.

Artificial Harmonics:
After the note is fretted normally, the pick hand lightly touches the string at the fret (in parentheses) with one finger while plucking with another.

Mutes

Muffled Strings: A percussive sound is produced by laying the fret hand across the strings without depressing them to the fretboard, and then striking the strings with the pick hand.

Palm Mute (P.M.): The note is partially muted by the pick hand by lightly touching the string or strings just before the bridge.

Tremolos

Tremolo Picking: The string is picked down-and-up as rapidly as possible.

Vibrato

Pick the string as the fret finger or a tremolo bar rapidly rolls back and forth or bends up and down, making the note sound slightly higher and lower. An exaggerated vibrato can be achieved by rolling the fret finger a greater distance.

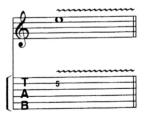

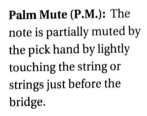

Slides

Slide: Pick the lower (first) note, then slide the fret finger up to sound the higher (second) note. The higher note is not picked again.

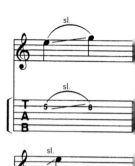

Long Slide: Strike the note during the slide up to the desired note.

Pick Slide: The edge of the pick slides down the entire string. A scratchy, downward sound is produced.

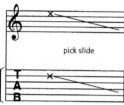

Tapping

Hammer-on: Pick the lower (first) note, then hammer-on (tap down) the higher (second) note with another finger. Pick only the first note. These notes are always played on the same string.

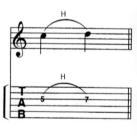

Pull-off: Place both fret fingers on the two notes to be played. Pick the higher (first) note, then pull-off (raise up) the finger of the higher note while keeping the lower note fretted. Pick only the first note.

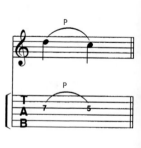

Tapping: Tap down on the fretted string with the index or middle finger of the pick hand. This is usually followed by a pull-off to sound the lower note.

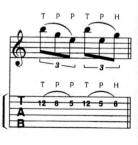

RANGES

*Notes in parentheses are those which may be
included on some instruments, but not all.*

Woodwinds

Piccolo (in C)

written: sounds one octave higher:

Flute

(sounds as written)

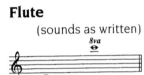

Alto Flute in G

written: sounds a perfect fourth lower:

Bass Flute

written: sounds one octave lower:

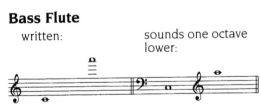

Oboe

(sounds as written)

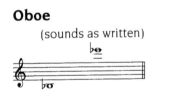

English Horn (in F)

written: sounds a perfect fifth lower:

Heckelphone (in C) (infrequently used)

written: sounds one octave
                                lower:

Bassoon

(sounds as written)

Contrabassoon

written: sounds one octave
                                lower:

E♭ Clarinet

written: sounds a minor
                                third higher:

B♭ Clarinet

written: sounds a major
                                second lower:

A Clarinet

written: sounds a minor
                                third lower:

E♭ Alto Clarinet

written: sounds a major
                                sixth lower:

E♭ Contra Alto Clarinet

written: sounds one octave
                                plus a major sixth
                                lower:

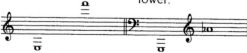

B♭ Contrabass Clarinet

written: sounds one octave
                            plus a major ninth
                            lower:

E♭ Sopranino Saxophone (infrequently used)

written: sounds a minor
                            third higher:

B♭ Soprano Saxophone

written: sounds a major
                            second lower:

E♭ Alto Saxophone

written: sounds a major
                            sixth lower:

B♭ Tenor Saxophone

written: sounds a major
                            ninth lower:

E♭ Baritone Saxophone

written: sounds one octave
                            plus a major sixth
                            lower:

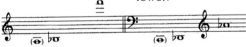

B♭ Bass Saxophone (infrequently used)

written: sounds one octave
                            plus a major ninth
                            lower:

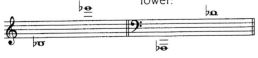

Soprano Recorder

written: sounds one octave higher:

Alto Recorder

(sounds as written)

Tenor Recorder

(sounds as written)

Bass Recorder

written: sounds one octave lower:

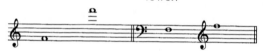

Brass

French Horn (in F)

written: sounds a perfect fifth lower:

Note: In many older compositions, horn parts written in bass clef sound a perfect fourth higher.

B♭ Tenor Wagner Tuba

written: sounds a major second lower:

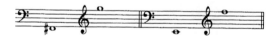

F Bass Wagner Tuba

written: sounds a perfect fifth lower:

Piccolo Trumpet in B♭ (infrequently used)

written: sounds a minor
seventh higher:

Piccolo Trumpet in A

written: sounds a major
sixth higher:

Trumpet in E♭

written: sounds a minor
third higher:

Trumpet in D (infrequently used)

written: sounds a major
second higher:

Trumpet in C
(sounds as written)

Trumpet in B♭ (Cornet)

written: sounds a major
second lower:

Bass Trumpet in E♭ (infrequently used)

written: sounds a major
sixth lower:

Bass Trumpet in C (infrequently used)

written: sounds one octave
lower:

Bass Trumpet in B♭ (infrequently used)

written: sounds a major
                  ninth lower:

Flugelhorn (in B♭)

written: sounds a major
                  second lower:

Alto Trombone (infrequently used)
(sounds as written)

Tenor Trombone
(sounds as written)

Bass Trombone
(sounds as written)

Baritone Horn (Euphonium) Treble Clef

written: sounds a major
                  ninth lower:

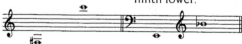

Baritone Horn (Euphonium) Bass Clef
(sounds as written)

Tuba
(sounds as written)

8va bassa┘

Stringed Instruments

Violin (sounds as written)

open strings: range:

Viola (sounds as written)

open strings: range:

Violoncello (Cello) (sounds as written)

open strings: range:

Double Bass (sounds one octave lower)

open strings: written range:

Guitar (sounds one octave lower)

open strings: written range:

Mandolin (sounds as written)

open strings: range:

Ukelele (sounds as written)

open strings: range:

Banjo (Five String)
(sounds one octave lower)

standard tuning
open strings: written range:

Banjo (Four-String Tenor)
(sounds one octave lower)

open strings: written range:

Percussion

Timpani (sounds as written)

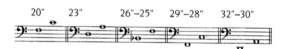

Glockenspiel (orchestra bells)

written: sounds two octaves
                         higher:

Xylophone

written: sounds one octave
                         higher:

Vibraphone
(sounds as written)

Chimes (tubular bells)
(sounds as written)*

* Because of complex overtones, some hear chimes as sounding an octave lower than written.

Marimba
(sounds as written)

Other Instruments

Accordion (sounds as written)

keyboard: bass   chords:
                   patterns:

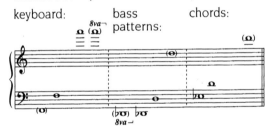

Celesta

written: sounds one
                            octave higher:

Piano (sounds as written)

Harp (sounds as written)

Harpsichord (sounds as written)

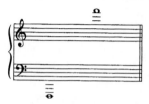

Harmonica—12-hole chromatic
(sounds as written)

Harmonica—10-hole diatonic in C
(sounds as written)

Voices

(with the exception of tenor, all sound as written)

Soprano

Alto

Tenor

written: sounds one octave
lower:

Baritone

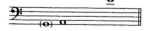

Bass